Turn Sales into Partnerships: The Definitive Guide to Consultative Selling

Copyright © 2024 Reginaldo Osnildo
All rights reserved.

PRESENTATION

INTRODUCTION TO CONSULTATIVE SELLING: MORE THAN SELLING, SOLVING

THE CONSULTATIVE SELLER'S MINDSET: THINKING LIKE A PARTNER

KNOWING YOUR CUSTOMER: THE FOUNDATION OF CONSULTING

EFFECTIVE COMMUNICATION: LISTENING TO SOLVE

DEVELOPING CUSTOMIZED SOLUTIONS: THE HEART OF CONSULTATIVE SELLING

BUILDING AND MAINTAINING TRUSTED RELATIONSHIPS

CONSULTATIVE NEGOTIATION: CLOSING WIN-WIN AGREEMENTS

OBJECTIONS MANAGEMENT IN CONSULTATIVE SALES

TOOLS AND TECHNOLOGIES FOR THE CONSULTATIVE SELLER

CONTINUOUS DEVELOPMENT: IMPROVING YOUR CONSULTATIVE SELLING SKILLS

30-DAY ACTION PLAN TO IMPLEMENT CONSULTATIVE SELLING

CONTINUING YOUR JOURNEY IN CONSULTATIVE SALES

REGINALDO OSNILDO

PRESENTATION

Welcome to "**Turn Sales into Partnerships: The Definitive Guide to Consultative Selling**", an essential guide designed to transform the way you see and sell in the modern world. If you are a sales professional aspiring to evolve from a traditional salesperson to a trusted advisor capable of creating significant value for your customers, this book is tailor-made for you.

Consultative selling is not just a sales strategy; it is a philosophy that puts the customer's needs at the center of all interactions. When you take this approach, you become more than a salesperson; becomes a successful partner for your client, someone capable of offering personalized solutions that precisely meet their needs and exceed their expectations.

This book is the result of my experience and perception accumulated over the years, synthesizing essential and updated knowledge that aims to facilitate your journey towards excellence in consultative sales. Each chapter has been carefully crafted to offer valuable insights, practical techniques, and strategic advice that will equip you to meet today's market challenges and stand out as a trusted advisor.

What can you expect from this book?

- **Clarity and depth:** Concepts explained clearly, with practical examples that illustrate how to apply them in everyday sales.

- **Focus on the reader:** All content is directed at you, facilitating immediate application of the strategies and techniques discussed.

- **Applied knowledge:** In addition to theory, this book offers a practical look at consultative selling, with an emphasis on actions you can take immediately.

- **Innovation and updating:** The latest strategies and tools in the field of consultative sales, ensuring you are ahead in your market.

As you progress from chapter to chapter, you will be invited to reflect on your current practices, challenged to think differently, and inspired to act in ways that transform your sales interactions into deep, meaningful relationships with your customers.

At the end of this journey, you will not only have gained in-depth knowledge about consultative selling, but you will also have developed the skills necessary to apply it successfully, ensuring long-term relationships and exceptional results for both you and your clients.

Ready to start this transformation?

Skip ahead to the next chapter, " **INTRODUCTION TO CONSULTATIVE SELLING: MORE THAN SELLING, SOLVING** ", and delve into the fascinating world of consultative selling, where solving is the key to building lasting relationships and generating ongoing success.

Let's go together on this journey of learning and growth, transforming not only the way we sell, but also how we create genuine value in each interaction. Welcome to the first step towards excellence in consultative selling.

Yours sincerely

Reginaldo Osnildo

INTRODUCTION TO CONSULTATIVE SELLING: MORE THAN SELLING, SOLVING

In today's world of sales, the traditional approach, focused simply on pushing products or services, is no longer as effective as it once was. Today's customers are more informed, demanding and expect more than just a transaction; they seek genuine solutions to their problems and trusted partners who can guide them through the complexities of their needs. This is where consultative selling comes in, a revolutionary method that transforms the salesperson-client dynamic and redefines sales success.

THE ESSENCE OF CONSULTATIVE SELLING

Consultative selling is a strategic approach that focuses on creating significant value for the customer by deeply understanding their needs, challenges and objectives. Unlike traditional selling, which often focuses on the product, consultative selling puts the customer at the center of the sales process. You, as a consultative salesperson, act more like an advisor or consultant than a salesperson in the traditional sense.

WHY CONSULTATIVE SALES?

- **Builds lasting relationships:** By focusing on customer needs and offering personalized solutions, you establish a foundation of mutual trust and respect, essential for long-term relationships.

- **Competitive differentiation:** In a saturated market, being able to position yourself as a trusted advisor can significantly differentiate you from the competition.

- **Mutually beneficial results:** Consultative selling seeks solutions that not only meet the customer's needs, but also create positive and sustainable results for both customer and seller.

THE PILLARS OF CONSULTATIVE SALES

- **Deep customer understanding:** This involves research,

active listening and the ability to ask the right questions to reveal not only what the customer says they need, but also their unspoken needs.

- **Customized solutions:** Based on customer understanding, you develop solutions that directly align with their challenges and goals.

- **Effective communication:** This means conveying value clearly, educating the customer about possible solutions and guiding the conversation so that the customer feels involved and valued.

- **Partnership relationship:** Consultative selling is, in essence, the building of a long-term relationship, where the seller is seen as a strategic partner in the customer's success.

STARTING WITH CONSULTATIVE SELLING

Switching to a consultative selling approach requires a change in both mindset and practice. This means cultivating curiosity, empathy and patience, as well as developing listening and analytical skills. You must be prepared to invest the time and effort to truly understand your customers and their needs, which in turn will allow you to offer truly personalized and effective solutions.

Embracing consultative selling can be a challenging but incredibly rewarding journey. By becoming a sales consultant, you not only improve your sales opportunities, but you also contribute significantly to your customers' success.

I invite you now to move on to the next chapter, " **THE CONSULTATIVE SELLER'S MINDSET: THINKING LIKE A PARTNER**," where we will explore the mental and emotional characteristics necessary to become an effective consultative seller. You will discover how empathy, curiosity and a genuine customer focus are crucial to this transformation. Together, we'll uncover what it really means to think and act like a true partner with your customers.

THE CONSULTATIVE SELLER'S MINDSET: THINKING LIKE A PARTNER

Becoming a successful consultative salesperson goes far beyond adopting new sales techniques or learning about new products and services. The essence of this transformation lies in adopting a new mindset, a new way of thinking and relating to your customers. This chapter is dedicated to exploring the mental and emotional characteristics that form the foundation of consultative selling, empowering you to become a true partner to your customers.

EMPATHY: THE HEART OF THE CONSULTATIVE SALESPERSON

Empathy is the ability to understand and share another person's feelings, putting yourself in their shoes and seeing the world through their eyes. In the context of consultative selling, empathy allows you to deeply understand your customers' needs, concerns, and goals, even those they may not be able to express directly. Being empathetic makes it easier to build trust and shows your customer that you are truly interested in helping them achieve their goals, not just closing a sale.

CURIOSITY: THE INQUISITIVE MIND

Curiosity is another cornerstone of the consultative sales mindset. It motivates you to ask deep questions, seek to fully understand your client's context, and explore the roots of their challenges. A curious consultative salesperson is always learning, not only about their own product or service, but also about the market, industry trends, and most importantly, about each customer they interact with. This inquisitive approach helps you identify unique opportunities to create value in ways that neither you nor the customer could have initially imagined.

FOCUS ON THE CUSTOMER: BEYOND SALES

Unlike traditional selling, which often focuses on the salesperson's sales objectives, consultative selling puts the focus on the customer's success. This means understanding that your customer's success is your success. Such an approach requires a genuine desire to help the customer overcome their challenges and achieve their goals, even if that means recommending a solution that does not immediately involve closing a sale. Customer focus promotes a lasting partnership and mutual trust, which are fundamental to long-term success.

ADAPTABILITY: NAVIGATING CHANGES

The market is always changing, as are the needs of your customers. Being adaptive means having the ability to adjust your strategies and approaches based on new information, customer feedback and market changes. An effective consultative salesperson is resilient and flexible, ready to evolve with their customers and the circumstances in which they operate.

CULTIVATING THE CONSULTATIVE SALESMAN'S MINDSET

Adopting the consultative sales mindset doesn't happen overnight. It is a continuous process of personal and professional development. It requires practice, reflection and, above all, a genuine commitment to your clients' success. By cultivating empathy, curiosity, customer focus, and adaptability, you will equip yourself to not only be a more effective salesperson, but also to become an indispensable partner to your customers.

Now that we understand the importance of adopting the right mindset, the next step is learning how to apply that mindset to truly understand your customers. In the next chapter, " **KNOWING YOUR CUSTOMER: THE FOUNDATION OF CONSULTING** ", we will explore techniques and strategies to deepen your understanding of customers, allowing you to offer truly personalized and effective solutions. Get ready to dive into the world of your customers and discover how you can become an even more effective consultant, transforming sales relationships into lasting successful partnerships.

KNOWING YOUR CUSTOMER: THE FOUNDATION OF CONSULTING

The foundation of any successful consultative selling relationship is a deep understanding of the customer. This chapter is dedicated to uncovering how you can truly get to know your customers, going beyond the superficial to uncover their real needs, challenges, and goals. This not only allows you to offer customized solutions that resonate with their specific needs, but also helps build a relationship of trust and partnership.

THE IMPORTANCE OF KNOWING YOUR CUSTOMER

Knowing your customer is not just about knowing the name of the company, the sector they operate in or what they have purchased in the past. It's about understanding the motivations underlying your needs, the specific challenges you face in your industry, and the long-term goals you want to achieve. This in-depth knowledge is what differentiates a consultative salesperson from a traditional salesperson.

HOW TO KNOW YOUR CUSTOMER

- **Deep research:** Before meeting with a client, spend time researching. This includes reviewing the company's website, its social media posts, industry publications, and any other sources that can offer insights into its challenges and goals.

- **Active listening:** During customer interactions, practice active listening. This means listening not just to what is said, but also how it is said and what is not being said. Active listening helps you capture important nuances about your customer's needs and wants.

- **Open-ended questions:** Ask questions that encourage the customer to share more about their needs and goals. Open-ended questions start with "how," "why," and "what" and are powerful tools for deepening your understanding of your customer.

- **Empathy and perspective:** Try to put yourself in your customer's shoes, understanding their concerns and challenges from their perspective. This not only helps you identify more effective solutions, but also build a stronger connection with the customer.

- **Continuous feedback:** Maintain a feedback loop with your customers where you can continually learn about their changing needs, emerging challenges, and how your solutions are helping them achieve their goals.

WHY THIS IS CRUCIAL

Understanding your customer is the basis for offering truly personalized solutions. Without this in-depth knowledge, proposed solutions may not fully meet the customer's needs or may fail to solve the core problem. Furthermore, getting to know your client reinforces the relationship of trust, showing that you value their success as much as your own.

THE PATH TO CUSTOMIZED SOLUTIONS

Knowing your customer is the essential first step to becoming an effective consultative seller. With this knowledge, you can develop custom solutions that not only solve customer problems but also help them achieve their long-term goals. This customer-centric approach is the key to building long-lasting, trusting partnership relationships.

With a deep understanding of your customer in hand, the next step is to learn how to communicate your solutions effectively. In the next chapter, " **EFFECTIVE COMMUNICATION: LISTENING TO SOLVE** ", we will explore how advanced communication skills, especially active listening, are key to identifying opportunities, creating effective solutions and strengthening relationships with your customers. Get ready to deepen your communication skills and take your customer interactions to the next level.

EFFECTIVE COMMUNICATION: LISTENING TO SOLVE

Effective communication is the backbone of consultative selling. This chapter explores how mastering the art of communication can transform your interactions with customers, allowing you to not only understand their needs on a deeper level but also present your solutions in a way that truly resonates with them. Here, the focus is on active listening, an essential skill that paves the way for effective solutions and lasting trusting relationships.

ACTIVE LISTENING AS A FUNDAMENTAL TOOL

Active listening goes beyond hearing the words that are spoken; it involves understanding the full message being conveyed, including the subtext and feelings behind the words. This requires full attention, patience, and the ability to read nonverbal cues such as body language and tone of voice.

HOW TO PRACTICE ACTIVE LISTENING

- **Be present:** During conversations, eliminate distractions. This means turning off electronic devices, maintaining eye contact, and demonstrating with your body language that you are fully engaged in the conversation.

- **Reflect and clarify:** To ensure you understand correctly, reflect on what was said and ask for clarification when necessary. This can be done by repeating what you understood in your own words and asking if you understood correctly.

- **Encourage continuity:** Use gestures and words that encourage the client to continue talking, showing interest and valuing their contributions. Simple phrases like "That's interesting, can you tell me more about that?" can open doors to deeper understanding.

- **Watch for non-verbal cues:** Attention to non-verbal cues can offer valuable insights into how the customer really feels, allowing you to adjust your approach as needed.

WHY EFFECTIVE COMMUNICATION IS CRUCIAL

Effective communication allows you to identify and understand the customer's true needs, which are often not expressed directly. Not only does this increase your chances of developing solutions that meet those needs more effectively, but it also helps build a trusting relationship by showing the customer that their concerns are heard and valued.

PRESENTING SOLUTIONS: THE ART OF COMMUNICATING VALUE

Once you have identified customer needs, the next step is to communicate how your solution can meet those needs. This involves:

- **Customization:** Tailor your presentation to reflect how your solution specifically meets the customer's challenges and goals.

- **Highlighted benefits:** Focus on how your solution's features translate into tangible benefits for the customer, rather than simply listing features.

- **Stories and examples:** Use case studies or success stories to illustrate how your solution has helped similar customers, making the value more tangible.

STRENGTHENING RELATIONSHIPS THROUGH COMMUNICATION

Mastering effective communication and active listening not only improves your ability to identify and solve customer problems, it also strengthens bonds of trust and mutual respect. By demonstrating that you are truly committed to customer success, you establish yourself as a trusted advisor, paving the way for long-lasting, collaborative relationships.

Now that we understand the importance of effective

communication and active listening, the next chapter, "**DEVELOPING CUSTOMIZED SOLUTIONS: THE HEART OF CONSULTATIVE SELLING**", will dive into how to utilize these skills to develop and present solutions that perfectly align with the specific needs of the customer. client. Get ready to explore how to transform collected information into innovative, personalized solutions that drive value for your customers.

DEVELOPING CUSTOMIZED SOLUTIONS: THE HEART OF CONSULTATIVE SELLING

The essence of consultative selling lies in the ability to develop and present customized solutions that meet the specific needs of each client. This chapter will guide you through the process of creating these solutions, from deeply understanding the customer's needs to presenting a proposal that resonates directly with their goals and challenges. Here, collected information and effective communication converge to create solutions that not only solve problems, but also lay the foundation for a lasting, trusting relationship.

UNDERSTANDING CUSTOMER NEEDS

The first step in developing a custom solution is to have a comprehensive understanding of the customer's needs. This involves:

- **Detailed analysis:** Using the information collected during your interactions with the customer to identify not only their explicit needs, but also those implicit ones that may not have been directly expressed.

- **Identification of challenges and objectives:** Understand the specific challenges the client faces and what objectives they want to achieve with the proposed solution.

CREATING THE SOLUTION

With a clear understanding of the customer's needs, the next step is to create a solution that is truly personalized. This involves:

- **Tailor-made solutions:** Develop a proposal that perfectly aligns with the client's needs, challenges and objectives, ensuring that each aspect of the solution offers direct value.

- **Focus on benefits:** Make sure the solution emphasizes the specific benefits the customer will obtain, translating features and functionalities into tangible results.

- **Innovation and creativity:** Apply creative thinking to develop innovative solutions that not only meet current customer needs, but also anticipate future demands.

PRESENTING THE SOLUTION

Presenting the solution is as crucial as its creation. Here, the way you communicate the solution can make all the difference. This involves:

- **Clear and persuasive communication:** Explain how the solution works clearly and how it aligns with the customer's needs and goals, using language that resonates with them.

- **Demonstration of value:** Clearly show the value that the solution offers, ideally through examples or case studies that demonstrate success in similar situations.

- **Feedback and adjustments:** Be open to customer feedback on the proposed solution and willing to make adjustments as necessary to ensure it perfectly meets their needs.

THE ART OF CREATING REAL VALUE

Developing customized solutions is the art of creating real value for your customers. By aligning your proposals with each client's specific needs, you not only increase your chances of sales success, but you also establish a solid foundation for a long-term relationship based on trust and partnership. This is the heart of consultative selling: the ability to be more than a salesperson, but a true consultant who contributes significantly to the client's success.

With the personalized solution presented, the next step is to solidify and maintain a trusting relationship with the customer. In the next chapter, " **BUILDING AND MAINTAINING TRUSTED RELATIONSHIPS** ," we will explore strategies for building, nurturing, and maintaining long-term relationships with your clients, ensuring a long-lasting, mutually beneficial partnership. Get ready to learn how trust is the key to unlocking the true potential of your customer relationships.

BUILDING AND MAINTAINING TRUSTED RELATIONSHIPS

Consultative selling transcends the immediate transaction, aiming to build and maintain long-term relationships based on trust, respect and mutual value. This chapter focuses on the strategies and practices you can adopt to not only build but also sustain trusting relationships with your customers, ensuring a lasting partnership that benefits both parties.

THE FOUNDATION OF TRUST

Trust is the foundation of any successful relationship, especially in consultative selling. Building trust starts with:

- **Integrity and honesty:** Be transparent in all your interactions. This means being honest about what your solution can and cannot do, setting realistic expectations from the start.

- **Consistency:** Show consistency in your actions and in keeping promises. Reliability lays a solid foundation for trust.

- **Customer appreciation:** Genuinely demonstrate that you value the customer and their success by going beyond sales to offer support and guidance.

STRATEGIES FOR BUILDING LASTING RELATIONSHIPS

- **Continuous understanding:** Keep striving to understand changing customer needs and goals, adapting your solutions as necessary. This shows that you are committed to the customer's long-term success.

- **Proactive communication:** Maintain open lines of communication, providing regular updates and being available to answer questions and concerns. Proactive communication reinforces the idea that you are always on your customer's side.

- **Exceptional support and service:** Provide exceptional customer support, helping you resolve issues quickly and efficiently. Excellent customer service is key to building trust.

MAINTAINING CONFIDENCE OVER TIME

Building trust is just the beginning; maintaining it over time is what sustains lasting relationships. That includes:

- **Adaptability:** Being willing to adapt to changes in customer needs and the market environment, showing that you are a flexible and attentive partner.

- **Continuous learning:** Be open to feedback and use it as an opportunity to learn and improve. This demonstrates a commitment to continued excellence.

- **Celebrate successes:** Recognize and celebrate successes, big and small, reinforcing the value of partnership and encouraging a shared team feeling.

THE VALUE OF TRUSTING RELATIONSHIPS

Trusting relationships are the cornerstone of consultative selling. Not only do they facilitate repeat sales and referrals, they also create an environment where innovative, collaborative solutions can flourish. By investing time and effort into building and maintaining these relationships, you establish yourself not just as a salesperson, but as a trusted advisor and long-term partner in customer success.

Now that we've established the importance of building and maintaining trusting relationships, the next chapter, " **CONSULTATIVE NEGOTIATION: CLOSING WIN-WIN AGREEMENTS** ", will explore how to take these trusting relationships to the negotiation table, securing agreements that benefit both parties. This chapter will provide strategies for effective negotiations that strengthen the partnership between you and your clients, creating fertile ground for mutual success.

CONSULTATIVE NEGOTIATION: CLOSING WIN-WIN AGREEMENTS

Consultative negotiation is a natural extension of the principles of consultative selling, where the focus is on creating solutions that result in mutual benefits for all parties involved. This chapter offers an in-depth look at how to conduct negotiations effectively, ensuring that you and your clients reach agreements that satisfy both parties, further strengthening the relationship of trust and partnership.

PRINCIPLES OF CONSULTATIVE NEGOTIATION

- **Preparation:** Before entering into any negotiation, it is crucial to be well prepared. This means fully understanding your client's needs, challenges and objectives, as well as being clear about the limits and possibilities of your offer.

- **Focus on value:** Focus on discussing the value your solution brings to the customer, rather than just price or terms. By focusing on value, you change the conversation from a zero-sum game to a discussion about mutual benefits.

- **Active listening:** Employ active listening techniques during negotiation to truly understand the client's concerns and goals. This can reveal areas of alignment and opportunities for creative solutions.

STRATEGIES FOR WIN-WIN NEGOTIATIONS

- **Explore common interests:** Identify and build on common interests. When both parties recognize common ground, it becomes easier to find solutions that meet everyone's needs.

- **Flexibility:** Be willing to be flexible in your approach. This may involve adjusting terms, customizing packages, or offering alternatives that meet the client's objectives without compromising its core principles.

- **Clear and assertive communication:** Be clear and assertive about what you can offer, always maintaining an open and collaborative stance. This helps you set realistic expectations and build a positive negotiation environment.

MANAGING DIFFERENCES AND OBJECTIONS

In any negotiation, differences and objections may arise. Managing them effectively is key to keeping negotiations on the right track.

- **Validation:** Acknowledge the customer's concerns without necessarily agreeing with them. This demonstrates respect for the customer's point of view and keeps the discussion productive.

- **Investigation:** Use questions to explore the customer's objections more deeply, seeking to understand the root of the problem. This may reveal non-obvious solutions.

- **Creative proposals:** Offer creative solutions that solve customer concerns in unexpected ways. This can turn objections into opportunities.

BUILDING PARTNERSHIPS THROUGH NEGOTIATION

Successful negotiations in the context of consultative selling are not just about closing a deal, but about strengthening and deepening the partnership relationship with the client. By taking a consultative approach to negotiation, you demonstrate an ongoing commitment to client success, laying a solid foundation for future collaboration.

Effective objection management is essential in the consultative selling process. In the next chapter, " **OBJECTIONS MANAGEMENT IN CONSULTATIVE SALES** ", we will explore how to approach and overcome objections in a consultative manner, using them as opportunities to deepen your understanding of customer needs and reinforce the value proposition of your solution. This chapter will equip you with the tools and techniques needed to turn objections into levers for building even stronger relationships with your customers.

OBJECTIONS MANAGEMENT IN CONSULTATIVE SALES

Objection management is a crucial step in the consultative selling process. Objections are not simply barriers to the sale; they offer a unique opportunity to deepen your understanding of customer needs and concerns, reinforcing the value proposition of your solution. This chapter covers effective techniques for handling objections in a consultative manner, turning potential obstacles into stepping stones to sales success.

UNDERSTANDING THE OBJECTIONS

- **Identification:** The first step is to correctly identify the objection. Not every hesitation is a direct objection, and understanding the true concern behind a comment is critical.

- **Classification:** Objections generally fall into categories such as price, need, urgency or trust. Classifying the objection helps you determine the best way to address it.

TECHNIQUES FOR MANAGING OBJECTIONS

- **Active listening and empathy:** Demonstrate empathy and use active listening to fully understand the customer's objection. Not only does this show respect for the customer's perspective, but it can also reveal important information to overcome the objection.

- **Clarification:** Objections often arise from misunderstandings or lack of information. Asking the customer to elaborate on their concern can clarify the problem and pave the way for a solution.

- **Validation:** Validating the customer's objection shows that you take their concerns seriously. This doesn't mean agreeing, but recognizing that your concerns are valid and deserve attention.

OVERCOMING OBJECTIONS WITH SOLUTIONS

- **Strengthening the value proposition:** Use the objection as an opportunity to reinforce the value proposition of your solution, highlighting how it specifically addresses the concerns raised.

- **Customization:** If possible, offer adjustments or customizations to your solution that directly address the customer's objection.

- **Evidence and testimonials:** Presenting concrete evidence, such as case studies or customer testimonials, can help overcome objections, especially those related to the effectiveness or value of the solution.

TRANSFORMING OBJECTIONS INTO OPPORTUNITIES

- **Deepening the relationship:** Each objection overcome is a chance to deepen the relationship with the customer, showing that you are committed to their long-term success.

- **Valuable feedback:** Objections provide valuable feedback that can be used to improve your offering and sales approach, making them more aligned with market needs.

THE ART OF RESILIENCE IN CONSULTATIVE SELLING

Effective objection management in consultative selling is an art that requires resilience, empathy and a deep understanding of the customer's needs. By approaching objections not as barriers, but as opportunities to strengthen the relationship and value proposition, you position yourself not just as a salesperson, but as a true consultative partner for your customers.

After exploring objection management, in the next chapter, " **TOOLS AND TECHNOLOGIES FOR THE CONSULTATIVE SELLER** ", we will explore the latest solutions that can support the consultative selling process, from CRMs to data analytics platforms and communications tools, to help you to become even more effective in your consultative selling practices.

TOOLS AND TECHNOLOGIES FOR THE CONSULTATIVE SELLER

In today's digital era, consultative salespeople are increasingly supported by a range of advanced tools and technologies. These solutions not only facilitate the effective management of customer relationships, but also provide valuable insights that can enhance the consultative selling process. This chapter explores the essential tools and technologies that can transform the way you engage with your customers, optimizing your efforts and maximizing success.

CRM (CUSTOMER RELATIONSHIP MANAGEMENT) SYSTEMS

- **Importance:** CRM tools are essential for managing detailed information about customers, recording past interactions and planning future sales actions. They allow for a deeper understanding of the customer's needs and history, facilitating a more personalized sales approach.

- **Recommendations:** Salesforce, HubSpot and Zoho CRM are examples of robust systems that offer advanced functionalities, adaptable to the needs of different profiles of consultative sellers.

DATA ANALYSIS PLATFORMS

- **Importance:** Data analysis allows consultative salespeople to identify patterns, trends and opportunities within their target market. With this information, it is possible to adjust sales strategies to better meet customer needs.

- **Recommendations:** Google Analytics, Tableau and Microsoft Power BI are powerful tools that can help analyze large volumes of data, providing actionable insights to improve your sales strategies.

COMMUNICATION AND COLLABORATION TOOLS

- **Importance:** Maintaining clear and efficient communication with customers is essential in consultative selling. Communication and collaboration tools facilitate this process, allowing for more dynamic and productive interactions.

- **Recommendations:** Slack, Microsoft Teams and Zoom are platforms that offer versatile communication solutions, from instant messaging to video conferencing, supporting effective collaboration with clients and internal teams.

MARKETING AUTOMATION PLATFORMS

- **Importance:** Marketing automation helps nurture leads and customers with personalized content and targeted campaigns based on their behavior and preferences, reinforcing the consultative approach of understanding and meeting specific customer needs.

- **Recommendations:** Marketo , Mailchimp , and HubSpot all offer automation capabilities that can be integrated into your CRM, enabling consistent and relevant communication with your customer base.

ONLINE EDUCATION AND TRAINING TOOLS

- **Importance:** Continuous training is vital to stay up to date with best consultative selling practices and market trends. Online education and training tools allow easy access to educational resources and training programs.

- **Recommendations:** LinkedIn Learning, Coursera , and Udemy offer a wide range of courses and educational materials, ranging from consultative selling skills to the effective use of specific tools and technologies.

TECHNOLOGY AS AN ALLY OF THE CONSULTATIVE SELLER

The tools and technologies mentioned in this chapter are just the tip of the iceberg. The key to maximizing their potential is to select them based on how they can support and improve your consultative selling approach. By implementing these technology solutions, you can significantly increase your effectiveness by offering solutions that not only meet but exceed customer expectations.

Improving your consultative selling skills is an ongoing process. In the next chapter, " **CONTINUOUS DEVELOPMENT: IMPROVING YOUR CONSULTATIVE SELLING SKILLS** ", we'll explore resources, best practices, and strategies for ongoing professional development, ensuring you stay ahead on your journey as a successful consultative seller.

CONTINUOUS DEVELOPMENT: IMPROVING YOUR CONSULTATIVE SELLING SKILLS

In the dynamic world of sales, continuous development is crucial to maintaining relevance and effectiveness. For consultative sellers, this means always learning, adapting and improving your skills. This chapter explores strategies and resources you can use to continue growing professionally, ensuring your consultative selling skills not only stay sharp but also evolve with market trends and customer needs.

INVESTING IN FORMAL EDUCATION AND TRAINING

- **Courses and certifications:** Look for specialized courses in consultative selling and related areas, such as communication, negotiation, and data analysis. Certifications from recognized institutions can not only deepen your knowledge but also reinforce your credibility.

- **Workshops and seminars:** Attending workshops and seminars offers a double advantage: practical learning and networking opportunities. These events are ideal platforms to exchange experiences and absorb new ideas.

PRACTICAL LEARNING THROUGH EXPERIENCE

- **Customer feedback:** View customer feedback as a learning opportunity. Evaluate the feedback you receive to identify areas for improvement and adjust your approaches accordingly.

- **Mentoring and coaching:** Finding an experienced mentor or coach can accelerate your development, offering valuable insights based on real experiences and personalized guidance.

STAYING UP TO DATE WITH MARKET TRENDS

- **Continuous reading:** Stay informed about the latest market trends, new technologies and consultative sales practices through books, blogs, podcasts and industry magazines.

- **Social networks and professional forums:** Engage with

relevant online communities. Professional social networks and forums are excellent resources for sharing knowledge, asking questions, and staying up to date with current discussions in the field of consultative selling.

REFLECTIVE PRACTICE AND SELF-ASSESSMENT

- **Sales diary:** Keeping a diary of your sales interactions can help you reflect on what works and what can be improved. Use it to record successful strategies, challenges faced, and lessons learned.

- **Regular self-assessment:** Set aside time regularly to evaluate your performance, set personal and professional development goals, and monitor your progress. This can help keep your growth in line with your career aspirations.

THE LEARNING JOURNEY NEVER ENDS

The path to becoming a master of consultative selling is a continuous journey of learning and improvement. Investing in your development not only enhances your skills and knowledge, but also ensures that you can continue to deliver exceptional value to your customers. By embracing continuous development, you prepare yourself not only to meet current demands, but also to anticipate and respond to the future needs of the market and your customers.

Now that we've explored the knowledge bases and strategies for continued development, the next chapter will provide a step-by-step guide: " **30-DAY ACTION PLAN TO IMPLEMENT CONSULTATIVE SELLING** ." This plan is designed to help you put the principles of consultative selling into practice, turning theory into action and beginning your transformation into a successful consultative seller.

30-DAY ACTION PLAN TO IMPLEMENT CONSULTATIVE SELLING

Implementing a consultative selling approach requires more than just understanding its principles; It requires action and commitment to incorporate these practices into your daily sales routine. This chapter presents a detailed 30-day action plan designed to help you begin your consultative selling journey, transforming concepts into effective practices and improving your interactions with customers.

DAY 1-5: SELF-ASSESSMENT AND PREPARATION

Day 1: Assess your current skills

Take an honest inventory of your current sales skills. Identify areas of strength and areas in need of development.

Day 2-3: Set clear goals

Based on the self-assessment, set specific goals for what you want to achieve with consultative selling.

Day 4-5: Familiarize yourself with tools and resources

Choose CRM tools, data analytics platforms, and learning resources that will support your consultative selling journey.

DAY 6-10: EDUCATION AND SKILLS DEVELOPMENT

Day 6-7: Study the principles of consultative selling

Dedicate these days to deepen your understanding of consultative selling through readings, online courses or workshops.

Day 8-10: Develop specific skills

Focus on developing essential skills for consultative selling, such as active listening, customer needs analysis, and negotiation techniques.

DAY 11-20: PRACTICAL APPLICATION

Day 11-15: Practice with feedback

Apply consultative selling techniques in customer interactions. Ask for feedback from colleagues, mentors, or even clients to improve your approach.

Day 16-20: Adjustment and personalization

Use the feedback you receive to adjust your approach. Start personalizing your sales interactions based on each customer's specific needs.

DAY 21-25: REFINEMENT AND DEEPENING

Day 21-22: Analysis of success stories

Study consultative selling success stories to understand how the principles were effectively applied.

Day 23-25: Continuous improvement

Identify areas for continuous improvement. Consider how you can further integrate consultative selling practices into your sales process.

DAY 26-30: ASSESSMENT AND FUTURE PLANNING

Day 26-27: Evaluate your progress

Evaluate your progress against the goals you set at the beginning. Reflect on what worked well and what can be improved.

Day 28-30: Action plan for the future

Develop an action plan for the coming months. Include specific goals, strategies for achieving them, and how you will continue to utilize and improve your consultative selling skills.

This 30-day action plan is just the beginning of your consultative selling journey. Successful implementation requires continued dedication, reflection and adaptation. By committing to continuous improvement and putting these practices into action, you will be well positioned to become an effective consultative salesperson, capable of building meaningful relationships with clients and generating exceptional results for both of you.

With the foundations of consultative selling established and an action plan in progress, the next step is to continue the learning and improvement process. Stay engaged with new features, keep seeking feedback, and always be open to adjusting your strategies as you grow and evolve as a consultative seller.

CONTINUING YOUR JOURNEY IN CONSULTATIVE SALES

You've reached the end of this guide, but your consultative selling journey is just beginning. The beauty of consultative selling lies in its ability to adapt and grow with you and your customers. This final chapter is dedicated to looking to the future, considering how you can continue to develop your skills, adapt to market changes, and most importantly, create lasting value for your customers.

REFLECTING ON THE JOURNEY

Revisit and revise:

Regularly return to the goals you set at the beginning of your journey. Are they still relevant? What have you achieved and what is still pending?

Continuously reviewing your progress is crucial for sustained growth. Use the insights you gain to adjust your goals and strategies.

CONTINUOUS IMPROVEMENT

Education and learning:

Learning never stops. Keep looking for new information, tools and techniques that can enrich your consultative selling approach.

Attend workshops, seminars and courses. Interacting with other professionals can offer new perspectives and inspiration.

Adapting to changes:

The market is constantly evolving, as are the needs of its customers. Stay up to date with industry trends and be ready to adapt your approach as needed.

Use technology to your advantage. New and emerging tools and platforms can offer innovative ways to connect with and serve your customers.

BUILDING LASTING RELATIONSHIPS

In addition to the sale:

Continue to nurture the relationships you've built with your customers. Remember, consultative selling is about long-term partnerships.

Be present even after the sale is complete. Offer ongoing support and check in regularly to ensure solutions continue to meet your customers' needs.

TAKING A STEP FURTHER

Contribute to the community:

Share your knowledge and experiences with others. Whether through blogs, lectures or mentoring, contributing to the sales community enriches the profession as a whole.

Engage in discussion forums and professional social networks. Sharing insights can open doors to new opportunities and collaborations.

Consultative selling is more than a methodology; It's a philosophy that puts customers' needs at the heart of every business interaction. By taking this approach, you not only achieve sales success, but you also help your customers thrive, which in turn builds a solid foundation for your own continued growth and development.

Remember, the consultative selling journey is a road that unfolds as you go. Every customer, every sale and every challenge is an opportunity to learn, improve and make a difference. With passion, dedication and a commitment to excellence, you can reach incredible heights and make a significant impact in the world of sales.

Keep exploring, learning and growing. The world of consultative selling is always evolving, and now you are equipped with the tools, knowledge and mindset needed to navigate this journey with confidence and success. Stay curious, resilient, and always focused on the value you can create for your customers. The future is bright for those who commit to being masters of consultative selling.

With this chapter, we conclude the book "**Turn Sales into Partnerships: The Definitive Guide to Consultative Selling**". This guide is designed to be your companion on the journey to becoming a successful consultative seller, equipping you with the strategies, knowledge, and inspiration you need to transform your sales practices and build meaningful, long-term relationships with your customers.

As we turn the final page of this journey together, I sincerely hope that the learnings shared here have touched your heart and sparked new perspectives. If this book has brought you any value, I kindly ask that you take a few moments to leave a review on Amazon. Your words not only help me grow and hone my craft, but they also guide other readers in their quests for knowledge and inspiration. Your opinion is a valuable gift, both for me and for the community of readers looking for stories that transform. I sincerely thank you for sharing this journey with me and I hope we can meet again in the pages of a new adventure.

REGINALDO OSNILDO

Hello, I'm Reginaldo Osnildo, author and innovator in the areas of sales, technology, and communication strategies. My experience ranges from the academic environment, as a professor and researcher at the University of Southern Santa Catarina, to practice as a strategist at Grupo Catarinense de Rádios. With a PhD in sales narratives and digital convergence, and a master's degree in storytelling and social imaginary, I bring my readers a unique fusion of theory and practice. My goal is to provide knowledge in a simple, practical and didactic language, encouraging direct application in personal and professional life.

Yours sincerely

Reginaldo Osnildo

+55 48 991913865

reginaldoosnildo@gmail.com

www.ingramcontent.com/pod-product-compliance
Lightning Source LLC
Chambersburg PA
CBHW070421230526
45471CB00006B/2914